Burning City

Burning City

NEW POEMS

by

STEPHEN VINCENT BENÉT

DECORATIONS BY CHARLES CHILD

FARRAR & RINEHART

INCORPORATED

On Murray Hill   *New York*

To
JOHN FARRAR

Acknowledgment

Acknowledgment is made to "The Atlantic Monthly," "Common Sense," "The New Yorker," "The New Republic," "The Saturday Review of Literature," and "The Yale Literary Magazine" for permission to reprint poems contained in this volume.

Contents

ONE

TWO

THREE

ONE

Notes to Be Left in a Cornerstone

This is for you who are to come, with Time,
And gaze upon our ruins with strange eyes.

So, always, there were the streets and the high, clear light
And it was a crowded island and a great city;
They built high up in the air.

I have gone to the museum and seen the pictures.

And yet shall not know this body. It was other;
Though the first sight from the water was even so,
The huge blocks piled, the giants standing together,
Noble with plane and mass and the squareness of stone,
The buildings that had skeletons like a man
And nerves of wire in their bodies, the skyscrapers,
Standing their island, looking toward the sea.
But the maps and the models will not be the same.
They cannot restore that beauty, rapid and harsh,
That loneliness, that passion or that name.

Yet the films were taken?

                              Most carefully and well,
But the skin is not the life but over the life.
The live thing was a different beast, in its time,

3

And sometimes, in the fall, very fair, like a knife sharpened
On stone and sun and blue shadow. That was the time
When girls in red hats rode down the Avenue
On the tops of busses, their faces bright with the wind,
And the year began again with the first cool days.
All places in that country are fair in the fall.

You speak as if the year began with the fall.

It was so. It began then, not with the calendar.
It was an odd city. The fall brought us new life,
Though there was no festival set and we did not talk of it.

That seems to me strange.
It was not strange, in that city.
We had four seasons: the fall of the quick, brief steps
Ringing on stone and the thick crowds walking fast,
The clear sky, the rag of sunset beyond great buildings,
The bronze flower, the resurrection of the year.
The squirrels ran in the dry Park, burying nuts.
The boys came from far places with cardboard suitcases.
It is hard to describe, but the lights looked gay at night then
And everything old and used had been put away.
There were cheap new clothes for the clerks and the clerks'
        women.
There was frost in the blood and anything could begin.
The shops were slices of honeycomb full of honey,
Full of the new, glassed honey of the year.
It seemed a pity to die then, a great pity.
The great beast glittered like sea-water in the sun,

His heart beating, his lungs full of air and pride,
And the strong shadow cutting the golden towers.

Then the cold fell, and the winter, with grimy snow,
With the overcoatless men with the purple hands
Walking between two signboards in the street
And the sign on their backs said "Winter" and the soiled
    papers
Blew fretfully up and down and froze in the ice
As the lukewarm air blew up from the grated holes.
This lasted a long time, till the skin was dry
And the cheeks hot with the fever and the cough sharp.
On the cold days, the cops had faces like blue meat,
And then there was snow and pure snow and tons of snow
And the whole noise stopping, marvellously and slowly,
Till you could hear the shovels scraping the stone,
Scritch-scratch, scritch-scratch, like the digging of iron mice.
Nothing else but that sound, and the air most pure,
Most pure, most fragrant and most innocent,
And, next day, the boys made dirty balls of the snow.

This season lasted so long we were weary of it.
We were very weary indeed when the spring came to us.
And it came.
I do not know how even yet, but there was a turning,
A change, a melting, a difference, a new smell
Though not that of any flower.
                      It came from both
Rivers, I think, or across them. It sneaked in
On a market truck, a girl in a yellow hat

5

With a pinched, live face and a bunch of ten-cent narcissus
And the sky was soft and it was easy to dream.
You could count the spring on your fingers, but it came.
Ah, brief it was in that city, but good for love!
The boys got their stick-bats out then, the youths and girls
Talked hoarsely under street lamps, late in the night.

And then it was tiger-summer and the first heat,
The first thunder, the first black pile of aching cloud,
The big warm drops of rain that spatter the dust
And the ripping cloth of lightning.
                                    Those were the hot
Nights when the poor lay out on the fire-escapes
And the child cried thinly and endlessly. Many streets
Woke very late in the night, then.
And barbarously the negro night bestrode
The city with great gold rings in his ears
And his strong body glistening with heat.
He had, I think, a phial in one hand
And from it took a syringe, dry as dust,
To dope tired bodies with uneasy sleep.
The backs of my hands are sweating with that sleep
And I have lain awake in the hot bed
And heard the fierce, brief storm bring the relief,
The little coolness, the water on the tongue,
The new wind from the river, dear as rain.

I have not studied the weather-reports intensively.
Should I do so?
                            You will not get it from weather-reports.
There was the drunkard's city and the milkman's,

6

The city of the starving and the fed,
The city of the night-nurse and the scrubbed wall.
All these locked into each other like sliding rings
And a man, in his time, might inhabit one of them
Or many, as his fate took him, but always, always,
There were the blocks of stone and the windows gazing
And the breath that did not stop. It was never quite still.
You could always hear some sound, though you forgot it,
And the sound entered the flesh and was part of it.

It was high but no one planned it to be so high.
They did not think, when they built so. They did not say,
"This will make life better, this is due to the god,
This will be good to live in." They said "Build!"
And dug steel into the rocks.
                              They were a race
Most nervous, energetic, swift and wasteful,
And maddened by the dry and beautiful light
Although not knowing their madness.
                              So they built
Not as men before but as demons under a whip
And the light was a whip and a sword and a spurning heel
And the light wore out their hearts and they died praising it.

And for money and the lack of it many died,
Leaping from windows or crushed by the big truck.
They shot themselves in washrooms because of money.
They were starved and died on the benches of subway-
    stations,

The old men, with the caved cheeks, yellow as lard,
The men with the terrible shoes and the open hands,
The eyeing and timid crowd about them gathered.
Yet it is not just to say money was all their god
Nor just to say that machine was all their god.
It is not just to say any one thing about them.
They built the thing very high, far over their heads.
Because of it, they gave up air, earth and stars.

Will you tell me about the people, if you please?

They are all gone, the workers on the high steel,
The best of their kind, cat-footed, walking on space,
The arcs of the red-hot rivet in the air;
They are gone with the empty, arrogant women of price,
The evening women, curried till their flesh shone;
With the big, pale baker, the flour in his creases,
Coming up to breathe from his hell on a summer night;
They are gone as if they were not.
The blue-chinned men of the hotel-lobbies are gone,
Though they sat like gods in their chairs;
Night-watchmen and cleaning-women and millionaires;
The maimed boy, clean and legless and always sitting
On his small, wheeled platform, by the feet of the crowd;
The sharp, sad newsmen, the hackers spinning their wheels;
The ardent, the shy, the brave;
The women who looked from mean windows, every day,
A pillow under their elbows, heavily staring;
They are gone, gone with the long cars and the short ones,

8

They have dropped as smoothly as coins through the slot of
    Time,
Mrs. Rausmeyer is gone and Mrs. Costello
And the girl at Goldstein & Brady's who had the hair.
Their lipsticks have made no mark on the evening sky.
It is long ago this all was. It is all forgotten.

And yet, you lie uneasy in the grave.

I cannot well lie easy in the grave.
All cities are the loneliness of man
And this was very lonely, in its time
(Sea-haunted, river-emblemed, o the gray
Water at ends of streets and the boats hooting!
The unbelievable, new, bright, girl moon!),
Most cruel also, but I walked it young,
Loved in it and knew night and day in it.
There was the height and the light. It was like no other.
When the gods come, tell them we built this out of steel,
Though men use steel no more.
And tell the man who tries to dig this dust,
He will forget his joy before his loneliness.

Short Ode

It is time to speak of these
Who took the long, strange journey overseas,
Who fell through the air in flames.
Their names are many. I will not name their names
Though some were people I knew;
After some years the ghost itself dies, too,
And that is my son's picture on the wall
But his girl has been long married and that is all.
They died in mud, they died in camps of the flu.
They are dead. Let us leave it so.
The ones I speak of were not forced, I know.
They were men of my age and country, they were young men
At Belleau, at the seaports, by the Aisne.
They went where their passion took them and are not.
They do not answer mockery or praise.

You may restore the days
They lived beneath and you may well restore
The painted image of that fabled war,
But not those faces, not the living ones
Drowned in the water, blown before the guns
In France or Belgium or the bitter sea
(And the foreign grave is far, and men use the name,

But they did not go for votes or the pay they got
Or the brave memorial speech by the D.A.R.)
It is far, the foreign grave. It is very far
And the time is not the same.
But certain things are true
Despite the time, and these were men that I knew,
Sat beside, walked beside,
In the first running of June, in the careless pride.
It is hard to think back, to find them, to see their eyes
And none born since shall see those, and the books are lies,
Being either praise or blame.
But they were in their first youth. It is not the same.
You, who are young, remember that youth dies.
Go, stranger, and to Lacedemon tell,
They were shot and rotted, they fell
Burning, on flimsy wings.
And yet it was their thought that they did well.
And yet there are still the presidents, the kings.

Litany for Dictatorships

For all those beaten, for the broken heads,
The fosterless, the simple, the oppressed,
The ghosts in the burning city of our time . . .

For those taken in rapid cars to the house and beaten
By the skilful boys, the boys with the rubber fists,
—Held down and beaten, the table cutting their loins,
Or kicked in the groin and left, with the muscles jerking
Like a headless hen's on the floor of the slaughter-house
While they brought the next man in with his white eyes
    staring.
For those who still said "Red Front!" or "God Save the
    Crown!"
And for those who were not courageous
But were beaten nevertheless.
For those who spit out the bloody stumps of their teeth
Quietly in the hall,
Sleep well on stone or iron, watch for the time
And kill the guard in the privy before they die,
Those with the deep-socketed eyes and the lamp burning.

For those who carry the scars, who walk lame—for those
Whose nameless graves are made in the prison-yard

And the earth smoothed back before morning and the lime
    scattered.

For those slain at once. For those living through months and
    years
Enduring, watching, hoping, going each day
To the work or the queue for meat or the secret club,
Living meanwhile, begetting children, smuggling guns,
And found and killed at the end like rats in a drain.

For those escaping
Incredibly into exile and wandering there.
For those who live in the small rooms of foreign cities
And who yet think of the country, the long green grass,
The childhood voices, the language, the way wind smelt then,
The shape of rooms, the coffee drunk at the table,
The talk with friends, the loved city, the waiter's face,
The gravestones, with the name, where they will not lie
Nor in any of that earth. Their children are strangers.

For those who planned and were leaders and were beaten
And for those, humble and stupid, who had no plan
But were denounced, but grew angry, but told a joke,
But could not explain, but were sent away to the camp,
But had their bodies shipped back in the sealed coffins,
"Died of pneumonia." "Died trying to escape."

For those growers of wheat who were shot by their own
    wheat-stacks,

For those growers of bread who were sent to the ice-locked
    wastes,
And their flesh remembers their fields.

For those denounced by their smug, horrible children
For a peppermint-star and the praise of the Perfect State,
For all those strangled or gelded or merely starved
To make perfect states; for the priest hanged in his cassock,
The Jew with his chest crushed in and his eyes dying,
The revolutionist lynched by the private guards
To make perfect states, in the names of the perfect states.

For those betrayed by the neighbours they shook hands with
And for the traitors, sitting in the hard chair
With the loose sweat crawling their hair and their fingers
    restless
As they tell the street and the house and the man's name.

And for those sitting at table in the house
With the lamp lit and the plates and the smell of food,
Talking so quietly; when they hear the cars
And the knock at the door, and they look at each other
    quickly
And the woman goes to the door with a stiff face,
Smoothing her dress.
             "We are all good citizens here.
We believe in the Perfect State."
                     And that was the last
Time Tony or Karl or Shorty came to the house
And the family was liquidated later.

14

It was the last time.

                        We heard the shots in the night
But nobody knew next day what the trouble was
And a man must go to his work. So I didn't see him
For three days, then, and me near out of my mind
And all the patrols on the streets with their dirty guns
And when he came back, he looked drunk, and the blood was
     on him.

For the women who mourn their dead in the secret night,
For the children taught to keep quiet, the old children,
The children spat-on at school.

                         For the wrecked laboratory,
The gutted house, the dunged picture, the pissed-in well,
The naked corpse of Knowledge flung in the square
And no man lifting a hand and no man speaking.

For the cold of the pistol-butt and the bullet's heat,
For the rope that chokes, the manacles that bind,
The huge voice, metal, that lies from a thousand tubes
And the stuttering machine-gun that answers all.

For the man crucified on the crossed machine-guns
Without name, without resurrection, without stars,
His dark head heavy with death and his flesh long sour
With the smell of his many prisons—John Smith, John Doe,
John Nobody—oh, crack your mind for his name!
Faceless as water, naked as the dust,
Dishonored as the earth the gas-shells poison

15

And barbarous with portent.

                        This is he.
This is the man they ate at the green table
Putting their gloves on ere they touched the meat.
This is the fruit of war, the fruit of peace,
The ripeness of invention, the new lamb,
The answer to the wisdom of the wise.
And still he hangs, and still he will not die,
And still, on the steel city of our years
The light fails and the terrible blood streams down.

We thought we were done with these things but we were
    wrong.
We thought, because we had power, we had wisdom.
We thought the long train would run to the end of Time.
We thought the light would increase.
Now the long train stands derailed and the bandits loot it.
Now the boar and the asp have power in our time.
Now the night rolls back on the West and the night is solid.
Our fathers and ourselves sowed dragon's teeth.
Our children know and suffer the armed men.

Ode to the Austrian Socialists

(FEBRUARY 12—FEBRUARY 15, 1934)

They shot the Socialists at half-past five
In the name of victorious Austria.
                                        The sky
Was blue with February those four cold days
And the little snow lay lightly on the hard ground.
(Vienna's the laughing city of tunes and wine,
Of *Schlagobers* and starved children . . . and a great
    ghost . . .)
They had called the general strike but the plans went wrong
Though the lights failed, that first night.
                                        It is odd to turn
The switch by your bed and have no lamp go on
And then look out of the windows at the black street
Empty, except for a man with a pistol, running.
We have built our cities for lights and the harsh glare
And, when the siren screams at the winter stars,
It is only a fire, an ambulance, nothing wrong,
Just part of the day. You can walk to the corner store
And never duck at a bullet. The lights are there
And, if you see a man with a pistol, running,
You phone the police or wait for tomorrow's papers.
It is different, with the lights out and the shots beginning. . . .

These were ordinary people.
The kind that go to the movies and watch parades,
Have children, take them to parks, ride in trolley cars,
The workmen at the next bench, the old, skilful foreman;
You have seen the backs of their necks a million times
In any crowd and forgotten—seen their faces,
Anonymous, tired, good-humored, faces of skill.
(The quick hands moving deftly among machines,
Hands of the baker and the baker's wife,
Hands gloved with rubber, mending the spitting wire,
Hands on controls and levers, big, square-palmed hands
With the dint of the tool upon them,
Dull, clumsy fingers laboring a dull task
And others, writing and thoughtful, or sensitive
As a setter's mouth.) You have seen their hats and their shoes
Everywhere, in every city. They wear no costumes.
Their pockets have lint in them, and tobacco-dust.
Their faces are the faces of any crowd.

It was Monday when this began.
                              They were slow to start it
But they had been pushed to the wall. They believed in peace,
Good houses, meetings, elections and resolutions,
Not the sudden killing in corners, the armored cars
Sweeping the square, the bombs and the bloody heads,
But they'd seen what happened next door, in another country,
To people who believed in peace and elections
And the same tide was rising here. They could hear the
    storm.

18

They took to their guns at last, in the workmen's quarters,
Where they'd built the houses for peace and the sure future.

The houses were tall and fine,
Great blocks of manstone, built by people for people,
Not to make one man rich. When you do not build
To make one man rich, you can give people light and air,
You can have room to turn round—room after the day—
You can have books and clean water and healthy sleep,
A place for children to grow in.
All over the world men knew about those houses.

Let us remember Karl Marx Hof, Goethe Hof,
The one called Matteoti and all the rest.
They were little cities built by people for people.
They were shelled by six-inch guns.
                                        It is strange to go
Up the known stairs to the familiar room
And point the lean machine-gun out of the window,
Strange to see the black of that powder upon your hands. . . .

They had hidden arms against need but they could not find
    them
In many cases, being ordinary people.
The other side was much readier—Fey and Dollfuss
And all the shirts were quite ready.
                                When you believe
In parks and elections and meetings and not in death,
Not in Caesar,
It is hard to realize that the day may come

19

When you send your wife and children down to the cellar
To be out of the way of shells, and mount the known
Countable stairs to the familiar room,
The unfamiliar pistol cold in your fist
And your mouth dry with despair.
                              It is hard to think
In spite of all oppression, all enmity,
That that is going to happen.
And so, when it does happen, your plans go wrong.
(White flags on the Karl Marx Hof and the Goethe Hof
And the executions, later.)
                        A correspondent
Of the British press remarked, when the thing was done
And they let him in to see it, that on the whole
The buildings were less damaged than you'd expect
From four days' bullets. True, he had seen, before,
A truckload of undertakers and cheap, pine coffins
Go to the disputed district.
But the buildings stood, on the whole. They had built them
    well.

These were ordinary people and they are dead.
Dead where they lived, by violence, in their own homes,
Between the desk and the door and the kitchen chair,
Dead in the courtyards where the children played
(The child's jaw smashed by a bullet, the bloody crib,
The woman sprawled like a rag on the clean stairs)
Uncaesarlike, unwarlike, merely dead.

Dead, or in exile many, or afraid
(And those who live there still and wake in the night,

20

Remembering the free city)
Silent or hunted and their leaders slimed.
The communists said they would not fight but they fought
Four days of bitter February,
Ill-led, outnumbered, the radio blaring lies
And the six-inch guns against them and all hope gone,
Four days in the Karl Marx Hof and the Goethe Hof
And nobody knows yet how many dead
And sensible men give in and accept the flag,
The badge, the arm-band, the gag, the slave-tyranny,
The shining, tin peace of Caesar.
                              They were not sensible,
Four days of February, two years ago.

Bring no flowers here,
Neither of mountain nor valley,
Nor even the common flowers of the waste field
That still are free to the poor;
No wreaths upon these graves, these houseless graves;
But bring alone the powder-blackened brass
Of the shell-case, the slag of bullets, the ripped steel
And the bone-spattering lead,
Infertile, smelling acridly of death,
And heap them here, till the rusting of guns, for
      remembrance.

Do You Remember, Springfield?

(VACHEL LINDSAY, NOVEMBER 10, 1879—DECEMBER 5, 1931)

The Illinois earth is black
(Do you remember, Springfield?)
The State is shaped like a heart,
Shaped like an arrowhead.

The black earth goes deep down.
(Do you remember, Springfield?)
Three feet under the plow
You can find the black earth still.

The towns settled, the woods
Fine in the spring and autumn,
The waters large and rolling,
The black earth ready to hand.

Surely this earth, this air
Should bear the prophet-singers,
Minstrels like colts unbroken,
Minstrels of leaves and corn.

Baltimore gave a stone,
A stone to another singer

(Do you remember, Springfield?)
But that was in years gone by.

A cat to tear at his breast
And a glass to work him madness,
That was the gift to Poe:
But things are different here.

There are votes here to be bought
And rich men here to buy them;
What more could a poet ask
Of the streets where Lincoln strode?

The Board of Health is superb.
The ladies watchful and cultured.
What more could a poet need
Or the heart of man desire?

Gather the leaves with rakes,
The burning autumn, Springfield,
Gather them in with rakes
Lest one of them turn to gold.

A leaf is only a leaf,
It is worth nothing, in Springfield.
It is worth as little as song,
Little as light and air.

Trap the lark in the corn,
Let it tell of your bounty, Springfield.

If you burn its eyes with a wire
It still will sing for a space.

A man is another affair.
We understand that, in Springfield.
If he sings, why, let him sing
As long as we need not hear.

He came with singing leaves;
It was really most unfortunate.
The Lindsays and the Frazees
Are sturdy pioneer stock.

He came with broncos and clouds
And the cornsilk of the moonlight.
It is not a usual thing
In Springfield, Illinois.

We will show his room and his book
For that brings trade to the city.
We try to use everything.
If you like, you can see his grave.

His mouth is stopped with earth,
The deep, black earth of Springfield.
He will not sing any more.
It is fine earth for the mute.

Let us give the Arts their due
And Lincoln a marble courthouse.

Both are respectably dead.
They need not trouble us, now.

Break the colts to the plow
And make them pull their hearts out.
Break the broncos of dancing
And sell them for bones and hide.

Ode to Walt Whitman

(MAY 31, 1819—MARCH 26, 1892)

Now comes Fourth Month and the early buds on the trees.
By the roads of Long Island, the forsythia has flowered,
In the North, the cold will be breaking; even in Maine
The cold will be breaking soon; the young, bull-voiced
    freshets
Roar from green mountains, gorging the chilly brooks
With the brown, trout-feeding waters, the unlocked springs;
Now Mississippi stretches with the Spring rains. . . .

It is forty years and more,
The time of the ripeness and withering of a man,
Since you lay in the house in Camden and heard, at last,
The great, slow footstep, splashing the Third Month snow
In the little, commonplace street
—Town snow, already trampled and growing old,
Soot-flecked and dingy, patterned with passing feet,
The bullet-pocks of rain, the strong urine of horses,
The slashing, bright steel runners of small boys' sleds
Hitching on behind the fast cutters.
They dragged their sleds to the tops of the hills and yelled
The Indian yell of all boyhood, for pure joy
Of the cold and the last gold light and the swift rush down

Belly-flopping into darkness, into bedtime.
You saw them come home, late, hungry and burning-cheeked,
The boys and girls, the strong children,
Dusty with snow, their mittens wet with the silver drops of
    thawed snow.

All winter long, you had heard their sharp footsteps passing,
The skating crunch of their runners,
An old man, tied to a house, after many years,
An old man with his rivery, clean white hair,
His bright eyes, his majestic poverty,
His fresh pink skin like the first strawberry-bloom,
His innocent, large, easy old man's clothes
—Brown splotches on the hands of clean old men
At County Farms or sitting on warm park-benches
Like patient flies, talking of their good sons,
"Yes, my son's good to me"—
An old man, poor, without sons, waiting achingly
For spring to warm his lameness,
For spring to flourish,
And yet, when the eyes glowed, neither old nor tied.

All winter long there had been footsteps passing,
Steps of postmen and neighbors, quick steps of friends,
All winter long you had waited that great, snow-treading
    step,
The enemy, the vast comrade,
The step behind, in the wards, when the low lamp flickered
And the sick boy gasped for breath,

*"Lean on me!   Lean upon my shoulder!   By God, you shall
    not die!"*
The step ahead, on the long, wave-thundering beaches of
    Paumanok,
Invisible, printless, weighty,
The shape half-seen through the wet, sweet sea-fog of youth,
Night's angel and the dark Sea's,
The grand, remorseless treader,
Magnificent Death.

"Let me taste all, my flesh and my fat are sweet,
My body hardy as lilac, the strong flower.
I have tasted the calamus; I can taste the nightbane."

Always the water about you since you were born,
The endless lapping of water, the strong motion,
The gulls by the ferries knew you, and the wild sea-birds,
The sandpiper, printing the beach with delicate prints.
At last, old, wheeled to the wharf, you still watched the
    water,
The tanned boys, flat-bodied, diving, the passage of ships,
The proud port, distant, the people, the work of harbors. . . .

"I have picked out a bit of hill with a southern exposure.
I like to be near the trees. I like to be near
The water-sound of the trees."

Now, all was the same in the cluttered, three-windowed
    room,
Low-ceiled, getting the sun like a schooner's cabin,

The crowding photos hiding the ugly wall-paper.
The floor-litter, the strong chair, timbered like a ship,
The hairy black-and-silver of the old wolfskin;
In the back-yard, neither lilac nor pear yet bloomed
But the branch of the lilac swelling with first sap;
And there, in the house, the figures, the nurse, the woman,
The passing doctor, the friends, the little clan,
The disciple with the notebook who's always there.

All these and the pain and the water-bed to ease you
And you said it rustled of oceans and were glad
And the pain shut and relaxed and shut once more.

"Old body, counsellor, why do you thus torment me?
Have we not been friends from our youth?"

But now it came,
Slow, perceived by no others,
The splashing step through the grey, soft, Saturday rain,
Inexorable footstep of the huge friend.
"Are you there at last, fine enemy?
Ah, haste, friend, hasten, come closer!
Breathe upon me with your grave, your releasing lips!
I have heard and spoken; watched the bodies of boys
Flash in the copper sun and dive to green waters,
Seen the fine ships and the strong matrons and the tall
    axemen,
The young girls, free, athletic; the drunkard, retching
In his poor dream; the thief taken by officers;
The President, calm, grave, advising the nation;

The infant, with milk-wet lips in his bee-like slumber.
They are mine; all, all are mine; must I leave them, truly?
I have cherished them in my veins like milk and fruit.
I have warmed them at my bare breast like the eggs of
  pigeons.
The great plains of the buffalo are mine, the towns, the hills,
  the ship-bearing waters.
These States are my wandering sons.
I had them in my youth; I cannot desert them.
The green leaf of America is printed on my heart forever."

Now it entered the house, it marched upon the stair.
By the bedside the faces dimmed, the huge shoulder blotting
  them,
—It is so they die on the plains, the great, old buffalo,
The herd-leaders, the beasts with the kingly eyes,
Innocent, curly-browed,
They sink to the earth like mountains, hairy and silent,
And their tongues are cut by the hunter.
                                        Oh, singing tongue!
Great tongue of bronze and salt and the free grasses,
Tongue of America, speaking for the first time,
Must the hunter have you at last?

Now, face to face, you saw him
And lifted the right arm once, as a pilot lifts it,
Signalling with the bell,
In the passage at night, on the river known yet unknown,
—Perhaps to touch his shoulder, perhaps in pain—
Then the rain fell on the roof and the twilight darkened

And they said that in death you looked like a marvelous old,
 wise child.

2

It is Fourth Month now and spring in another century,
Let us go to the hillside and ask; he will like to hear us;
"Is it good, the sleep?"

       "It is good, the sleep and the waking.
I have picked out a bit of hill where the south sun warms me.
I like to be near the trees."

Nay, let him ask, rather.
"Is it well with you, comrades?
The cities great, portentous, humming with action?
The bridges mightily spanning wide-breasted rivers?
The great plains growing the wheat, the old lilac hardy,
 well-budded?
Is it well with these States?"

"The cities are great, portentous, a world-marvel,
The bridges arched like the necks of beautiful horses.
We had made the dry land bloom and the dead land
 blossom."

"Is it well with these States?"

"The old wound of your war is healed and we are one nation.
We have linked the whole land with the steel and the hard
 highways.

31

We have fought new wars and won them. In the French field
There are bones of Texarkana and Little Falls,
Aliens, our own; in the low-lying Belgian ground;
In the cold sea of the English; in dark-faced islands.
Men speak of them well or ill; they themselves are silent."

"Is it well with these States?"

"We have made many, fine new toys.
We—
There is a rust on the land.
A rust and a creeping blight and a scaled evil,
For six years eating, yet deeper than those six years,
Men labor to master it but it is not mastered.
There is the soft, grey, foul tent of the hatching worm
Shrouding the elm, the chestnut, the Southern cypress.
There is shadow in the bright sun, there is shadow upon the
      streets.
They burn the grain in the furnace while men go hungry.
They pile the cloth of the looms while men go ragged.
We walk naked in our plenty."

                                    "My tan-faced children?"

"These are your tan-faced children.
These skilled men, idle, with the holes in their shoes.
These drifters from State to State, these wolvish, bewildered
      boys
Who ride the blinds and the box-cars from jail to jail,
Burnt in their youth like cinders of hot smokestacks,

Learning the thief's crouch and the cadger's whine,
Dishonored, abandoned, disinherited.
These, dying in the bright sunlight they cannot eat,
Or the strong men, sitting at home, their hands clasping
    nothing,
Looking at their lost hands.
These are your tan-faced children, the parched young,
The old man rooting in waste-heaps, the family rotting
In the flat, before eviction,
With the toys of plenty about them,
The shiny toys making ice and music and light,
But no price for the shiny toys and the last can empty.
The sleepers in blind corners of the night.
The women with dry breasts and phantom eyes.
The walkers upon nothing, the four million.
These are your tan-faced children."

                "But the land?"

"Over the great plains of the buffalo-land,
The dust-storm blows, the choking, sifting, small dust.
The skin of that land is ploughed by the dry, fierce wind
And blown away, like a torrent;
It drifts foot-high above the young sprouts of grain
And the water fouls, the horses stumble and sicken,
The wash-board cattle stagger and die of drought.
We tore the buffalo's pasture with the steel blade.
We made the waste land blossom and it has blossomed.
That was our fate; now that land takes its own revenge,
And the giant dust-flower blooms above five States."

"But the gains of the years, who got them?"

"Many, great gains.
Many, yet few; they robbed us in the broad daylight,
Saying, 'Give us this and that; we are kings and titans;
We know the ropes; we are solid; we are hard-headed;
We will build you cities and railroads.'—as if *they* built
   them!
They, the preying men, the men whose hearts were like
   engines,
Gouging the hills for gold, laying waste the timber,
The men like band-saws, moving over the land.
And, after them, the others,
Soft-bodied, lacking even the pirate's candor,
Men of paper, robbing by paper, with paper faces,
Rustling like frightened paper when the storm broke.
The men with the jaws of moth and aphis and beetle,
Boring the dusty, secret hole in the corn,
Fixed, sucking the land, with neither wish nor pride
But the wish to suck and continue.
They have been sprayed, a little.
But they say they will have the land back again, these men."

"There were many such in my time.
I have seen the rich arrogant and the poor oppressed.
I have seen democracy, also. I have seen
The good man slain, the knave and the fool in power,
The democratic vista botched by the people,
Yet not despaired, loving the giant land,
Though I prophesied to these States."

34

"Now they say we must have one tyranny or another
And a dark bell rings in our hearts."

"Was the blood spilt for nothing, then?"

3

Under dry winter
Arbutus grows.
It is careless of man.
It is careless of man.

Man can tear it,
Crush it, destroy it;
Uproot the trailers,
The thumb-shaped leafings.

A man in gray clothes
May come there also,
Lie all day there
In weak spring sunlight.

White, firm-muscled,
The flesh of his body;
Wind, sun, earth
In him, possessing him.

In his heart
A flock of birds crying.
In his belly
The new grass growing.

In his skull
Sunlight and silence,
Like a vast room
Full of sunlight and silence.

In the lines of his palms
The roads of America,
In the knots of his hands
The anger of America.

In the sweat of his flesh
The sorrows of America,
In the seed of his loins
The glory of America.

The sap of the birch-tree
Is in his pelt,
The maple, the red-bud
Are his nails and parings.

He grows through the earth and is part of it like the roots
of new grass.

Little arbutus
Delicate, tinted,
Tiny, tender,
Fragile, immortal.

If you can grow,
A man can grow

Not like others
But like a man.

Man is a bull
But he has not slain you
And this man lies
Like a lover beside you.

Beside the arbutus,
The green-leaved Spring,
He lies like a lover
By his young bride,
In the white hour,
The white, first waking.

4

They say, they say, they say and let them say..
Call you a revolutionist—you were one—
A nationalist—you were one—a man of peace,
A man describing battles, an old fraud,
A Charlus, an adept self-advertiser,
A "good, gray poet"—oh, God save us all!
God save us from the memoirs and the memories!
And yet, they count. They have to. If they didn't
There'd be no Ph.Ds. And each disciple
Jealously guards his own particular store
Of acorns fallen from the oak's abundance
And spits and scratches at the other gatherers.
"I was there when he died!"

"He was not there when he died!"
"It was me he trusted, me! X got on his nerves!
He couldn't stand X in the room!"
                              "Y's well-intentioned
But a notorious liar—and, as for Z . . ."

So all disciples, always and forever.
—And the dire court at Longwood, those last years,
The skull of Sterne, grinning at the anatomists,
Poe's hospital-bed, the madness of the Dean,
The bright, coughing blood Keats wrote in to the girl,
The terrible corpse of France, shrunk, naked and solitary—
Oh, yes, you were spared some things.
Though why did Mrs. Davis sue the estate
And what did you mean when you said——
                              And who cares?
You're still the giant lode we quarry
For gold, fools' gold and all the earthy metals,
The matchless mine.
Still the trail-breaker, still the rolling river.

You and your land, your turbulent, seeking land
Where anything can grow.

And they have wasted the pasture and the fresh valley,
Stunk the river, shot the ten thousand sky-darkening pigeon
To build sham castles for imitation Medici
And the rugged sons of the rugged sons of death.
The slum, the sharecropper's cabin, the senseless tower,
The factory town with the dirty stoops of twilight,

The yelling cheapness, the bitter want among plenty,
But never Monticello, never again.

And there are many years in the dust of America
And they are not ended yet.

Far north, far north are the sources of the great river,
The headwaters, the cold lakes,
By the little sweet-tasting brooks of the blond country,
The country of snow and wheat,
Or west among the black mountains, the glacial springs.
Far north and west they lie and few come to them, few taste
    them,
But, day and night, they flow south,
By the French grave and the Indian, steadily flowing,
By the forgotten camps of the broken heart,
By the countries of black earth, fertile, and yellow earth and
    red earth,
A growing, a swelling torrent:
Rivers meet it, and tiny rivulets,
Meet it, stain it,
Great rivers, rivers of pride, come bowing their watery heads
Like muddy gift-bearers, bringing their secret burdens,
Rivers from the high horse-plains and the deep, green
    Eastern pastures
Sink into it and are lost and rejoice and shout with it, shout
    within it,
They and their secret gifts,
A fleck of gold from Montana, a sliver of steel from
    Pittsburgh,

A wheat-grain from Minnesota, an apple-blossom from
    Tennessee,
Roiled, mixed with the mud and earth of the changing
    bottoms
In the vast, rending floods,
But rolling, rolling from Arkansas, Kansas, Iowa,
Rolling from Ohio, Wisconsin, Illinois,
Rolling and shouting:
Till, at last, it is Mississippi,
The Father of Waters; the matchless; the great flood
Dyed with the earth of States; with the dust and the sun
    and the seed of half the States;
The huge heart-vein, pulsing and pulsing; gigantic; ever
    broader, ever mightier;
It rolls past broken landings and camellia-smelling woods;
    strange birds fly over it;
It rolls through the tropic magic, the almost-jungle, the
    warm darkness breeding the warm, enormous stars;
It rolls to the blue Gulf; ocean; and the painted birds fly.
The grey moss mixes with it, the hawk's feather has fallen
    in it,
The cardinal feather, the feather of the small thrush
Singing spring to New England,
The apple-pip and the pepper-seed and the checkerberry,
And always the water flowing, earthy, majestic,
Fed with snow and heat, dew and moonlight,
Always the wide, sure water,
Over the rotted deer-horn
The gold, Spanish money,
The long-rusted iron of many undertakings,

Over De Soto's bones and Joliet's wonder,
And the long forest-years before them, the brief years after,
The broad flood, the eternal motion, the restless-hearted
Always, forever, Mississippi, the god.

April, 1935.

TWO

For Those Who Are As Right As Any

"Spirit, they charge you that the time is ill.
The great wall sinks in the slime!"
"I am a spirit, still.
I do not walk with the time."

"The sky shivers, the king is a beast run wild,
The lords are sullen and base!"
"When the sun rose up in the East like a great child,
I saw the gold and the face."

"Come, draw your steel for the right, for the time wears on!
It is only a little way to Jerusalem!"
"I have seen the floating swan
And the lion, bloody with dawn,
I will make pictures of them."

"What, lift no sword in the battle?"

"I am swordless."

"No cause, no cry?"

"I am lordless."

"I am shadow, shadow that passes across the meadow
And goes its way."

"By God, against God, in our name, we will slay you, then!"

"Slay."

"And, when we have slain them all, we will build for men
The city called Marvelous, the glittering town,
And none shall be exalted or cast down
But all at ease, all hatreds reconciled."

*"I am air and I live. I live again and again.
I am wind and fire. But I am not reconciled."*

Girl Child

Like a flower, like a tulip,
So fresh, so hardy,
So slim, so hasting,
The nose tip-tilted,
The mouth her mother's,
The eyes brighter
Than rabbit's or squirrel's
Suddenly peering
From bough or burrow;
All this in motion,
Motion and swaying,
As if all life
Were a wave of ocean,
As if all life
Were the clean stalk springing
Brightly, greenly,
From earth unworn,
To sway with sunlight,
To drink clear freshets,
Swiftly, oh, swiftly
To swell its bubble,
The staunch red flower
Hardy and mortal,

The bright flag
On the new hill,
Mortal, gallant,
As a cockerel's cry.

To this child,
To all swift children,
My great thanks
For their clear honor,
The hound running,
The flying fire.

Old Man Hoppergrass

Flesh, if you were stone or tree,
I'd be happier with ye.

When I was young, I slept like stone,
When I was young, I grew like tree.
Now I lie, abed, alone,
And I wonder if 'tis me.

Wake at night and ease me
But it does not please me,
Stick I am, sick I am,
Apple pared to quick I am,
Woman-nursed and queer.
Once I had a sweet tooth,
A sharp tooth, a neat tooth,
Cocked my hat and winked my eye
As the pretty girls went by,
Pretty girls and punkin-pie—
Dear! oh, dear!

Old man's a hoppergrass
Kicking in the wheat.

Can't eat his fill,
Can't drink his will,

Can't climb his hill,
Can't have his Jill.

And, when he talks sense,
Relations say,
"Better let Father
Have his way."

A stone's a stone
And a tree's a tree,
But what was the sense
Of aging me?

It's no improvement
That *I* can see.

And the night's long
And the night-sleep brief
And I hear the rustle
Of the fallen leaf,
"Old man Hoppergrass,
Come and see!"

Well, I won't for a little,
Not while I'm me.

But the sun's not as hot
As it used to be.

Reply

It is a long time, yes,
Since the shape came out of the door
And took its food, and ate.
These things are not things to speak
Except alone or in sleep.
But I know it is a long time.
It is growing late.

You are saying that. You see
The first cat-paws of the dark
So hesitantly placed
They are barely shadow at all.
Nothing has changed, nothing.
But the sun is over the height.
There is different light on the wall.

It is a long time, long.
And so much wasted, yes.
And other men, oh, yes,
All the clever, better-placed men.
And so much bad work for bread,
The work that crawls in the hand
And that I would do again.

I do not explain. I say
It is all very true, yes.
It happened that way, yes.
It will not happen to you.
The stone spoke from the ground.
The water ran from the wound.
It happened that way, too.

A long time, very long, yes.
And the lateness beginning, yes.
And everything that you say
And the door shut with a weight.
O lightning, o forked bough,
Raining from the great sky,
The fire burns in the hand
Even this late.

Memory

They can have the names and the dates,
It will do them little service.
They can open the locked chest
And steal the wine and the gold.
There is nothing to be said
But this—the clasp of her body
Was better than milk to the child
Or wisdom to the old.

We die with our first breath.
And, if we die, what matter?
There was a ghost in the flesh,
A ghost that went and came.
Though the moon burn like a lamp
It will not be that brightness—
I said her name in my sleep,
Waking, I said her name.

The Lost Wife

In the daytime, maybe, your heart's not breaking,
For there's the sun and the sky and working
And the neighbors to give you a word or hear you,
But, ah, the long nights when the wind comes shaking
The cold, black curtain, pulling and jerking,
And no one there in the bed to be near you.

And worse than the clods on the coffin falling
Are the clothes in the closet that no one wears now
And the things like hairpins you're always finding.
And you wouldn't mind the ghost of her calling
As much as knowing that no one cares now
If the carpet fades when the sun gets blinding.

I look in the houses, when twilight narrows,
And in each a man comes back to a woman.
The thought of that coming has spurs to ride me.
—Death, you have taken the great like sparrows,
But she was so slight, so small, so human.
You might have left her to lie beside me.

Sparrow

Lord, may I be
A sparrow in a tree.

No ominous and splendid bird of prey
But something that is fearful every day
Yet keeps its small flesh full of heat and lightness.
Pigeons are better dressed and robins stouter,
The white owl has all winter in his whiteness
And the blue heron is a kingly dream
At evening, by the pale stream,
But, even in the lion's cage, in Zoos,
You'll find a sparrow, picking up the crumbs
And taking life precisely as it comes
With the black, wary eye that marks the doubter;
Squabbling in crowds, dust-bathing in the sun,
Small, joyous, impudent, a gutter-child
In Lesbia's bosom or December's chill,
Full of impertinence and hard to kill
As Queen Anne's lace and poppies in the wheat—
I won't pretend the fellow has a Muse
But that he has advice, and good advice,
All lovers know who've walked the city's street
And wished the stones were bread.

55

Peacocks are handsomer and owls more wise.
(At least, by all repute.)
And parrots live on flattery and fruit,
Live to great age. The sparrow's none of these.
The sparrow is a humorist, and dies.
There are so many things that he is not.
He will not tear the stag nor sweep the seas
Nor fall, majestical, to a king's arrow.
Yet how he lives, and how he loves in living
Up to the dusty tip of every feather!
How he endures oppression and the weather
And asks for neither justice nor forgiving!
Lord, in your mercy, let me be a sparrow!
His rapid heart's so hot.
And some can sing—song-sparrows, so they say—
And, one thing, Lord—the times are iron, now.
Perhaps you have forgot.
They shoot the wise and brave on every bough.
But sparrows are the last things that get shot.

Thanks

For these my thanks, not that I eat or sleep,
Sweat or survive, but that at seventeen
I could so blind myself in writing verse
That the wall shuddered and the cry came forth
And the numb hand that wrote was not my hand
But a wise animal's.
Then the exhaustion and the utter sleep.

O flagrant and unnecessary body,
So hard beset, so clumsy in your skill!
For these my thanks, not that I breathe and ache,
Talk with my kind, swim in the naked sea,
But that the tired monster keeps the road
And even now, even at thirty-eight,
The metal heats, the flesh grows numb again
And I can still go muttering down the street
Not seeing the interminable world
Nor the ape-faces, only the live coal.

For City Spring

Now grimy April comes again,
Maketh bloom the fire-escapes,
Maketh silvers in the rain,
Maketh winter coats and capes
Suddenly all worn and shabby
Like the fur of winter bears,
Maketh kittens, maketh baby,
Maketh kissing on the stairs.
Maketh bug crawl out of crack,
Maketh ticklings down the back
As if sunlight stroked the spine
To a hurdy-gurdy's whine
And the shower ran white wine.

April, April, sing cuckoo,
April, April, maketh new
Mouse and cockroach, man and wife,
Everything with blood and life;
Bloweth, groweth, flourisheth,
Danceth in a ragged skirt
On the very stoop of Death
And will take no mortal hurt.
Maketh dogs to whine and bound,

Maketh cats to caterwaul,
Maketh lovers, all around,
Whisper in the hall.

Oh, and when the night comes down
And the shrieking of the town
Settles to the steady roar
Of a long sea-beaten shore,
April hieth, April spieth
Everywhere a lover lieth,
Bringeth sweetness, bringeth fever,
Will not stop at "I would liever,"
Will not heed, "Now God a mercy!"
Turneth Moral topsy-versy,
Bringeth he and she to bed,
Bringeth ill to maidenhead,
Bringeth joyance in its stead.
By May, by May, she lieth sped,
Yet still we praise that crocus head,
April!

For City Lovers

Do not desire to seek who once we were,
Or where we did, or what, or in whose name.
Those buildings have been torn down. When the first
    wreckers
Tore the house open like a pack of cards
And the sun came in all over, everywhere,
They found some old newspapers and a cork
And footprints on the very dusty floor
But neither mouse nor angel.
                        Then even these
Went, even the little marks of shabby shoes,
The one sharp impress of the naked heel.

You cannot call us up there any more.
The number has been changed. There was a card
Downstairs, with names and such, under the bell.
But that's long gone. Yes, and we, they and you
And telegrams and flowers and the years
Went up and down these stairs, day after day,
And kept the stair-rail polished with our hands.
But we have moved to other neighborhoods.

Do not arraign that doorsill with your eyes
Nor try to make your hardened mind recall

How the old windows looked when they were lit
Or who the woman was on the third floor.
There are no ghosts to raise. There is the blank
Face of the stone, the hard line of the street,
The boys crying through twilight. That is all.

Go buy yourself a drink and talk about it.
Carry a humming head home through the rain.
But do not wear rosemary, touch cold iron,
Or leave out food before you go to bed.
For there's no fear of ghosts. That boy and girl
Are dust the sparrows bathe in, under the sun:
Under the virgin rock their bones lie sunken
Past pave and conduit and hidden waters
Stifled like unborn children in the darkness,
Past light and speech, cable and rooted steel,
Under the caissons, under the foundation.

Peace, peace, for there are people with those names
Somewhere or elsewhere, and you must not vex
Strangers with words about an old address.
But, for those others, do not be afraid.
They are beyond you. They are too deep down
For steel to pierce, for engines to uncover.
Not all the desperate splitters of the earth,
Nitro or air-drill or the chewing shovel
Shall ever mouth them up from where they lie.

Complaint of Body, the Ass, Against His Rider, the Soul

BODY

Well, here we go!
I told you that the weather looked like snow.
Why couldn't we have stayed there at the inn?
There was good straw and barley in the bin
And a grey jenny with a melting eye,
Neat-hoofed and sly—I rather like them sly—
Master a trader and a man of sense.
He likes his life and dinner. So do I.
Sleeps warm and doesn't try to cross a pass
A mountain-goat would balk at in his prime,
Where the hail falls as big as Peter's Pence
And every stone you slip on rolls a mile!
But that's not you, of course—that's not our style—
We're far too dandipratted and sublime!
Which of us is the ass?

Good ground, beyond the snow?
I've heard that little song before, you know.
Past cliff and ragged mount
And the wind's skinning-knife,
Far and forever far,

The water of the fount,
The water that is life
And the bright star?
Give me my water from a decent trough,
Not dabs of ice licked out of freezing stone
And, as for stars, why, let the stars alone,
You'll have us both in glory soon enough!

Alas, alack!
I'm carrying an idiot on my back.
I'm carrying Mr. Who to God Knows Where.
Oh, do not fix me with that burning stare
Of beauteous disdain!
I'm not a colt. I know my ass's rights.
A stall and fodder and sound sleep of nights.
One can't expect to live on sugarcane
But what's the sense, when one grows old and stiff,
Of scrambling up this devil-haunted cliff
To play hot cockles with the Northern Lights?
I'll balk, that's what I'll do!
And all the worse for you!
Oh, lash me if you like—I know your way—
Rake my poor sides and leave the bloody weal
Beneath your spurring steel.
My lungs are fire and my limbs are lead.

Go on ahead? I can't go on ahead.
Desert you in your need? Nay, master, nay.

Nay, master, nay; I grumble as I must
And yet, as you perceive, I do go on,

Grudging, impenitent and full of fear
And knowing my own death.
You have no fear because you have no breath.
Your silver essence knows nor cold nor heat.
Your world's beyond. My only world is here.
(Oh, the sweet rollings in the summer dust,
The smell of hay and thistles and the street,
The quick life, done so soon!)
You'll have your guerdon when the journey's done.
You'll play the hero where the wine is poured,
You and the moon—but I
Who served you well and shall become a bone,
Why do I live when it must be to die?
Why should I serve—and still have no reward?

SOUL

Your plaint is sound, yet I must rule you still
With bridle, bit and will.
For, without me, you are the child unborn
And the infertile corn.
I am not cruelty but I am he,
Drowning in sea, who yet disdains the sea,
And you that sea, that shore
And the brave, laboring oar,
Little upon the main,
That drives on reefs I know not of but does not drive in
    vain.
For I'm your master but your scholar, too,
And learn great things of you.

64

And, though I shall forsake you, nothing loth,
To grumble with the clods,
To sleep into the stone,
I'll answer for us both
When I stand up alone.
For it is part as your ambassador
I go before
To tell the gods who sit above the show,
How, in this world they never stoop to know,
Under what skies, against what mortal odds,
The dust grows noble with desire and pain,
And that not once but every day anew.

THREE

Metropolitan Nightmare

It rained quite a lot, that spring. You woke in the morning
And saw the sky still clouded, the streets still wet,
But nobody noticed so much, except the taxis
And the people who parade. You don't, in a city.
The parks got very green. All the trees were green
Far into July and August, heavy with leaf,
Heavy with leaf and the long roots boring and spreading,
But nobody noticed that but the city gardeners
And they don't talk.
                          Oh, on Sundays, perhaps, you'd notice:
Walking through certain blocks, by the shut, proud houses
With the windows boarded, the people gone away,
You'd suddenly see the queerest small shoots of green
Poking through cracks and crevices in the stone
And a bird-sown flower, red on a balcony,
But then you made jokes about grass growing in the streets
And politics and grass-roots—and there were songs
And gags and a musical show called "Hot and Wet."
It all made a good box for the papers. When the flamingo
Flew into a meeting of the Board of Estimate,
The new Mayor acted at once and called the photographers.
When the first green creeper crawled upon Brooklyn Bridge,
They thought it was ornamental. They let it stay.

69

There was the year the termites came to New York
And they don't do well in cold climates—but listen, Joe,
They're only ants and ants are nothing but insects.
It was funny and yet rather wistful, in a way
(As Heywood Broun pointed out in the *World-Telegram*)
To think of them looking for wood in a steel city.
It made you feel about life. It was too divine.
There were funny pictures by all the smart, funny artists
And Macy's ran a terribly clever ad:
"The Widow's Termite" or something.

                                   There was no
Disturbance. Even the Communists didn't protest
And say they were Morgan hirelings. It was too hot,
Too hot to protest, too hot to get excited,
An even, African heat, lush, fertile and steamy,
That soaked into bone and mind and never once broke.
The warm rain fell in fierce showers and ceased and fell.
Pretty soon you got used to its always being that way.

You got used to the changed rhythm, the altered beat,
To people walking slower, to the whole bright
Fierce pulse of the city slowing, to men in shorts,
To the new sun-helmets from Best's and the cops' white
      uniforms,
And the long noon-rest in the offices, everywhere.
It wasn't a plan or anything. It just happened.
The fingers tapped the keys slower, the office-boys
Dozed on their benches, the bookkeeper yawned at his desk.
The A. T. & T. was the first to change the shifts
And establish an official siesta-room,

But they were always efficient. Mostly it just
Happened like sleep itself, like a tropic sleep,
Till even the Thirties were deserted at noon
Except for a few tourists and one damp cop.
They ran boats to see the big lilies on the North River
But it was only the tourists who really noticed
The flocks of rose-and-green parrots and parrakeets
Nesting in the stone crannies of the Cathedral.
The rest of us had forgotten when they first came.

There wasn't any real change, it was just a heat spell,
A rain spell, a funny summer, a weather-man's joke,
In spite of the geraniums three feet high
In the tin-can gardens of Hester and Desbrosses.
New York was New York. It couldn't turn inside out.
When they got the news from Woods Hole about the Gulf
      Stream,
The *Times* ran an adequate story.
But nobody reads those stories but science-cranks.

Until, one day, a somnolent city-editor
Gave a new cub the termite yarn to break his teeth on.
The cub was just down from Vermont, so he took the time.
He was serious about it. He went around.
He read all about termites in the Public Library
And it made him sore when they fired him.
                              So, one evening,
Talking with an old watchman, beside the first
Raw girders of the new Planetopolis Building
(Ten thousand brine-cooled offices, each with shower)

He saw a dark line creeping across the rubble
And turned a flashlight on it.

"Say, buddy," he said,
"You better look out for those ants. They eat wood, you
    know,
They'll have your shack down in no time."

The watchman spat.
"Oh, they've quit eating wood," he said, in a casual voice,
"I thought everybody knew that."

—and, reaching down,
He pried from the insect jaws the bright crumb of steel.

Nightmare, with Angels

An angel came to me and stood by my bedside,
Remarking in a professorial-historical-economic and irritated
   voice,
"If the Romans had only invented a decent explosion-engine!
Not even the best, not even a Ford V-8
But, say, a Model T or even an early Napier,
They'd have built good enough roads for it (they knew how
   to build roads)
From Cape Wrath to Cape St. Vincent, Susa, Babylon and
   Moscow,
And the motorized legions never would have fallen,
And peace, in the shape of a giant eagle, would brood over
   the entire Western World!"
He changed his expression, looking now like a combination
   of Gilbert Murray, Hilaire Belloc and a dozen other
   scientists, writers, and prophets,
And continued, in angelic tones,
"If the Greeks had known how to coöperate, if there'd never
   been a Reformation,
If Sparta had not been Sparta, and the Church had been the
   Church of the saints,
The Argive peace like a free-blooming olive-tree, the peace
   of Christ (who loved peace) like a great, beautiful vine
   enwrapping the spinning earth!

Take it nearer home," he said.

"Take these Mayans and their star-clocks, their carvings and
their great cities.

Who sacked them out of their cities, drowned the cities with
a green jungle?

A plague? A change of climate? A queer migration?

Certainly they were skilful, certainly they created.

And, in Tenochtitlan, the dark obsidian knife and the
smoking heart on the stone but a fair city,

And the Incas had it worked out beautifully till Pizarro
smashed them.

The collectivist state was there, and the ladies very agree-
able.

They lacked steel, alphabet and gunpowder and they had to
get married when the government said so.

They also lacked unemployment and overproduction.

For that matter," he said, "take the Cro-Magnons,

The fellows with the big skulls, the handsome folk, the
excellent scribers of mammoths,

Physical gods and yet with the sensitive brain (they drew the
fine, running reindeer).

What stopped them? What kept us all from being Apollos
and Aphrodites

Only with a new taste to the nectar,

The laughing gods, not the cruel, the gods of song, not of
war?

Supposing Aurelius, Confucius, Napoleon, Plato, Gautama,
Alexander—

Just to take half a dozen—

Had ever realized and stabilized the full dream?

74

How long, O Lord God in the highest? How long, what
    now, perturbed spirit?"

He turned blue at the wingtips and disappeared as another
    angel approached me.
This one was quietly but appropriately dressed in cellophane,
    synthetic rubber and stainless steel,
But his mask was the blind mask of Ares, snouted for gas-
    masks.
He was neither soldier, sailor, farmer, dictator nor munitions-
    manufacturer.
Nor did he have much conversation, except to say,
"You will not be saved by General Motors or the pre-
    fabricated house.
You will not be saved by dialectic materialism or the
    Lambeth Conference.
You will not be saved by Vitamin D or the expanding
    universe.
In fact, you will not be saved."
Then he showed his hand:
In his hand was a woven, wire basket, full of seeds, small
    metallic and shining like the seeds of portulaca;
Where he sowed them, the green vine withered, and the
    smoke and the armies sprang up.

Nightmare Number Three

We had expected everything but revolt
And I kind of wonder myself when they started thinking—
But there's no dice in that now.

I've heard fellows say

They must have planned it for years and maybe they did.
Looking back, you can find little incidents here and there,
Like the concrete-mixer in Jersey eating the wop
Or the roto press that printed "Fiddle-dee-dee!"
In a three-color process all over Senator Sloop,
Just as he was making a speech. The thing about that
Was, how could it walk upstairs? But it was upstairs,
Clicking and mumbling in the Senate Chamber.
They had to knock out the wall to take it away
And the wrecking-crew said it grinned.

It was only the best

Machines, of course, the superhuman machines,
The ones we'd built to be better than flesh and bone,
But the cars were in it, of course . . .

and they hunted us

Like rabbits through the cramped streets on that Bloody
    Monday,
The Madison Avenue busses leading the charge.
The busses were pretty bad—but I'll not forget

The smash of glass when the Duesenberg left the show-room
And pinned three brokers to the Racquet Club steps
Or the long howl of the horns when they saw men run,
When they saw them looking for holes in the solid
      ground . . .

I guess they were tired of being ridden in
And stopped and started by pygmies for silly ends,
Of wrapping cheap cigarettes and bad chocolate bars
Collecting nickels and waving platinum hair
And letting six million people live in a town.
I guess it was that. I guess they got tired of us
And the whole smell of human hands.
                        But it was a shock
To climb sixteen flights of stairs to Art Zuckow's office
(Nobody took the elevators twice)
And find him strangled to death in a nest of telephones,
The octopus-tendrils waving over his head,
And a sort of quiet humming filling the air. . . .
Do they eat? . . . There was red . . . But I did not stop
      to look.
I don't know yet how I got to the roof in time
And it's lonely, here on the roof.
                  For a while, I thought
That window-cleaner would make it, and keep me company.
But they got him with his own hoist at the sixteenth floor
And dragged him in, with a squeal.
You see, they coöperate. Well, we taught them that
And it's fair enough, I suppose. You see, we built them.
We taught them to think for themselves.

It was bound to come. You can see it was bound to come.
And it won't be so bad, in the country. I hate to think
Of the reapers, running wild in the Kansas fields,
And the transport planes like hawks on a chickenyard,
But the horses might help. We might make a deal with the
    horses.
At least, you've more chance, out there.
                                    And they need us, too.
They're bound to realize that when they once calm down.
They'll need oil and spare parts and adjustments and tuning
    up.
Slaves? Well, in a way, you know, we were slaves before.
There won't be so much real difference—honest, there won't.
(I wish I hadn't looked into that beauty-parlor
And seen what was happening there.
But those are female machines and a bit high-strung.)
Oh, we'll settle down. We'll arrange it. We'll compromise.
It wouldn't make sense to wipe out the whole human race.
Why, I bet if I went to my old Plymouth now
(Of course you'd have to do it the tactful way.)
And said, "Look here! Who got you the swell French
    horn?"
He wouldn't turn me over to those police cars;
At least I don't think he would.
                              Oh, it's going to be jake.
There won't be so much real difference—honest, there
    won't—
And I'd go down in a minute and take my chance—
I'm a good American and I always liked them—
Except for one small detail that bothers me

And that's the food proposition. Because, you see,
The concrete-mixer may have made a mistake,
And it looks like just high spirits.
But, if it's got so they like the flavor . . . well . . .

1936

All night they marched, the infantrymen under pack,
But the hands gripping the rifles were naked bone
And the hollow pits of the eyes stared, vacant and black,
When the moonlight shone.

The gas mask lay like a blot on the empty chest,
The slanting helmets were spattered with rust and mold,
But they burrowed the hill for the machine-gun nest
As they had of old.

And the guns rolled, and the tanks, but there was no sound,
Never the gasp or rustle of living men
Where the skeletons strung their wire on disputed
    ground. . . .
I knew them, then.

"It is eighteen years," I cried. "You must come no more."
"We know your names. We know that you are the dead.
Must you march forever from France and the last, blind
    war?"
"*Fool! From the next!*" they said.